Our Baby from China
AN ADOPTION STORY

Nancy D'Antonio

ALBERT WHITMAN & COMPANY · Morton Grove, Illinois

If it weren't for my beloved Ariela Xiangwei, this book would not have been born. Thank you for the wealth of love, luck, and happiness you have bestowed upon our family.

This book is also dedicated to all the children adopted from China, who have transformed their parents' lives. Their spirits have enabled us to journey deep into our own selves and strengthened our sense of who we are. They remind us how far we were willing to go to experience parental love. And in return, their unconditional love for us has proved that it was worth the risk of traveling into the unknown waters of international and transracial adoption.

Thanks also to my husband, Garald Lee Farnham. Without his courage and steadfast support, we might not be living our dreams.

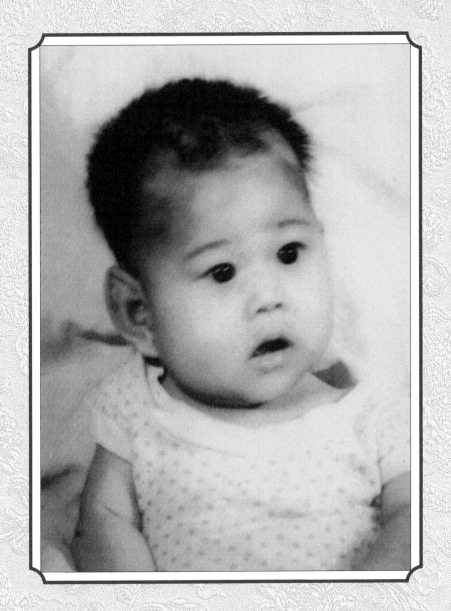

Once there was a little girl named Xiangwei (SHAN-way). She lived in China with a group of girls and boys who didn't have mothers or fathers to love them.

On the other side of the world, in America,
we were sad because we didn't have any children.
We heard that in China, there were many children
who needed families. So we wrote a letter to the
Chinese government asking to adopt a little girl.

After many months, your picture came in the
mail. We knew immediately that we loved you.

Soon we flew to China to meet you. On the way, we wanted to see the country where you were born. We visited several famous places. In Guilin, we saw beautiful mountains along the Li River.

In Beijing, the capital, we went to the Forbidden City. For hundreds of years, these buildings and gardens were the emperor's home. Only his family and servants were allowed to come inside.

North of Beijing, we walked along the Great Wall.
For over one thousand years, this mighty stone wall
with watchtowers protected the people from enemies.

We also visited the Lama Temple, a holy place in Beijing. There we lit incense and prayed for you.

Then we took the train to Ningbo, the town where you lived.

Since we couldn't speak or understand Chinese, Mrs. Zhao (Chow) and Mr. Wang helped us.

Your home was on the edge of town. The bus ride there was long and bumpy. At last we turned down a dirt road and crossed a bridge. Suddenly, we stopped in front of a building.

You were just a few steps away, waiting inside.

A friendly lady named Mrs. Sun took us upstairs. Your room was at the end of a long hall.

You were sitting in a wooden chair, playing with a rattle. You looked at us and then held out your arms.

We lifted you up together, hugged you, and held you tight. You were the most wonderful baby in the whole world! Now we were a family of three.

The next day, we met other Americans who were
adopting babies, too. They were as happy as we were.

We said hello to your friends:

Robin and Lingfang; Michael and Tingting;

Bill, Lin, and Meiying; and Renée and Hongxia.

Your Chinese caretakers had painted red dots
on your foreheads to bring you all good luck.

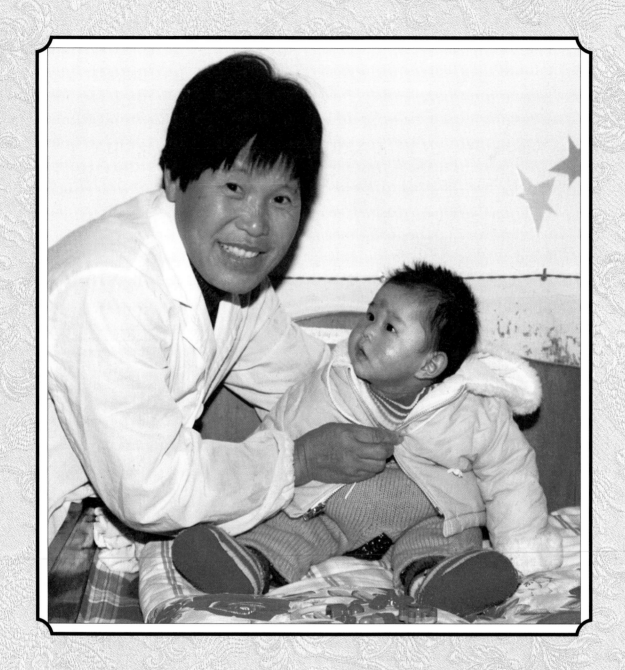

We met Mrs. Yang, one woman who had cared for you. She told us you came from a village near the East China Sea. She said you were happy and smart.

Next, we met with officials to get your adoption certificate and passport. We signed papers promising to take care of you always. We changed your name to Ariela Xiangwei because now you belonged to both America and China.

In Ningbo, we took you sightseeing.

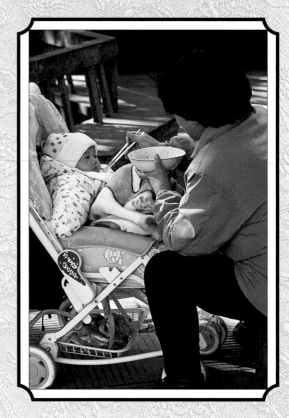

Everywhere we saw Chinese girls as beautiful as you.

Then Mommy fed you a bottle
and put you down for a nap.

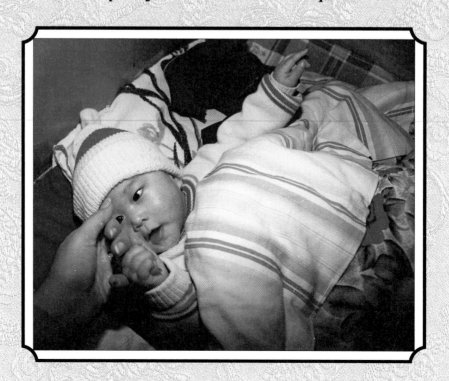

We stayed in Ningbo for ten days. On the last night, there was a banquet to honor our new families and the good friends we all had made in China. We would never forget the kindness of the Chinese people.

Now it was time to go home.

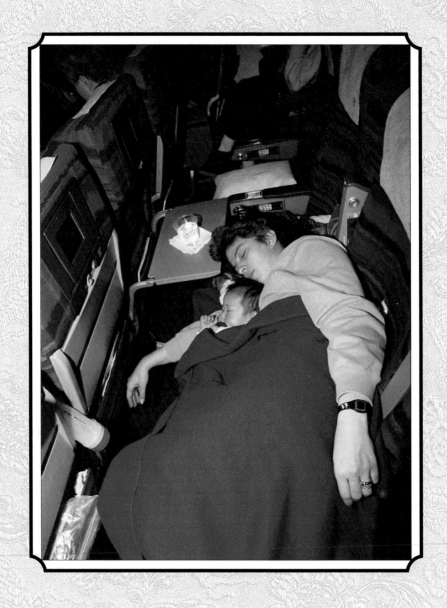

During the long airplane ride to
America, you slept in Mommy's arms.

Grandma and Grandpa D'Antonio met us at the airport. It was great to come home with our baby.

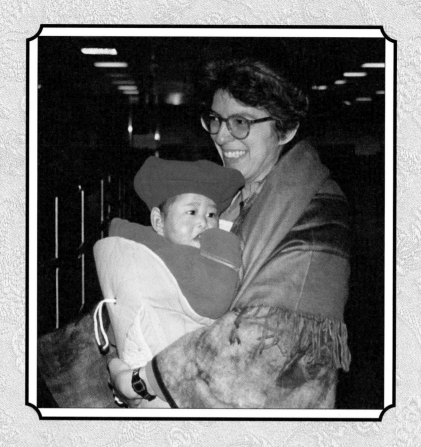

But we think you were a little scared. People were speaking a different language. The sights, sounds, and smells were not the same as they were in China.

Mommy held you close. She said that in America, there would be many new things to learn. And Mommy and Daddy would always be there to help you and love you.

At home, Grandma and Grandpa Farnham
and your new aunts, uncles, cousins,
and friends were eager
to meet you.

This was your forever family.

Library of Congress Cataloging-in-Publication Data

D'Antonio, Nancy.
Our baby from China: an adoption story / [written and photographed by]
Nancy D'Antonio.
p.   cm.
Summary: An American couple goes to China to adopt a baby.
ISBN 0-8075-6162-2
1. Intercountry adoption—United States—Juvenile literature. 2. Intercountry
adoption—China—Juvenile literature. [1. Adoption. 2. China—Description
and travel.] I. Title.
HV875.5.D36   1997   96-32327
362.7'34—DC21   CIP
                                                                            AC

Cover and interior design by Susan B. Cohn.
The text of this book is set in Benguiat.

PHOTO CREDITS: p. 2: Nancy Gutrich; p. 3: unknown Chinese official;
pp. 11-12: Angel Zhao; p. 15: Michael Niedenfuehr; p. 18 (top) and 20:
Garald Farnham; pp. 21-22: Karen McKinney; p. 23 (lower left): Scott
Schieber; p. 23 (lower center): United Photographic Industries. All other
photos: Nancy D'Antonio.